MIGRANT REMITTANCES AND HOUSEHOLD SURVIVAL IN ZIMBABWE

DANIEL TEVERA AND ABEL CHIKANDA

SERIES EDITOR:
PROF. JONATHAN CRUSH

SOUTHERN AFRICAN MIGRATION PROJECT
2009

Editorial Note

Information on remittance flows to and within Africa is notoriously unreliable, so SAMP embarked on a multi-country study to generate data on remittance volumes, channels and usage in Southern Africa. The Migration and Remittances Survey (MARS) was designed by a consortium of SAMP partners and researchers and implemented in several major migrant origin countries in the region. With the exception of Zimbabwe, most of the migrant movements and subsequent remittances flows are intra-regional. In the Zimbabwean case, about 60% of the migrants reside within the SADC region and 40% outside it, providing opportunities for comparison of the two migrant streams. The MARS methodology involved the representative sampling and interviewing of migrant-sending households in the countries of origin. A common survey instrument was used in all of the countries. To date, SAMP has published two regional overview papers with MARS data (Nos. 44 and 49). This is the second national study (following No. 43 on Mozambique). Although there have been changes in the volume of the migrant flow from Zimbabwe since 2005, we believe that the results of the MARS survey provide a unique window on the role of remittances in livelihoods and household survival in Zimbabwe. SAMP wishes to thank all of those involved in the design and implementation of MARS including the authors of this paper, Wade Pendleton, Bruce Frayne, Thuso Green, Hamilton Simelane, Fion de Vletter, Maxton Tsoka, Ndeyapo Nickanor, Selma Nangulah, Belinda Dodson, Sally Peberdy, Ntombi Msibi, Eugene Campbell, Kate Lefko-Everett, Krista House, David Dorey and Vincent Williams. Ashley Hill provided invaluable editorial assistance in the production of this paper. The MARS survey, and this publication, were made possible with financial assistance from DFID.

Published by Idasa, 6 Spin Street, Church Square, Cape Town, 8001, and Southern African Research Centre, Queen's University, Canada.

Copyright Southern African Migration Project (SAMP) 2009
ISBN 978-1-920118-92-1
First published 2009
Design by Bronwen Müller

CONTENTS

TABLES
PAGE

FIGURE   PAGE

EXECUTIVE SUMMARY

Migrant remittances are now recognised as an important source of global development finance and there is increasing evidence that international remittances have considerable developmental impacts. The contribution of remittances to GDP in many developing countries is significant and has shown a steady increase over the past decade. However, while there is a consensus that remittance flows to Africa are increasing, little attention has been paid to the impact of these transfers on poverty alleviation, primarily because of data deficiencies at the household level. Despite their obvious magnitude, accurate data on remittance flows to Zimbabwe is unavailable or inaccessible. In an attempt to address such data deficiencies, SAMP devised the household-level Migration and Remittances Survey (MARS) which was administered in several SADC countries, including Zimbabwe. The MARS study was implemented in Zimbabwe in 2005 and surveyed 723 urban and rural households.

The data generated by MARS is critical in at least three ways: (a) it quantifies the largely hidden economic value of labour migration from Zimbabwe; (b) it provides information on the significance of remittances to economic survival in a state undergoing massive formal sector decline; and (c) it provides information on the relationship between remittances and poverty alleviation at the household level. MARS allows us to do two things: first, to construct a profile of Zimbabwe's migrant population and, second, to answer basic questions about remittance origins, volumes, channels and use. With regard to the migrant profile MARS found the following:

- Nearly three quarters of the migrants (72%) identified in the survey had worked outside the country for 5 years or less. Only 7% had been working outside the country for over 10 years.
- The number of migrants per household varied between one and five. The majority (73%) were reliant on a single migrant, and another 21% had two.
- Nearly 60% of migrants were in neighbouring countries, primarily South Africa (32%), Botswana (16%) and Mozambique (5%). The other 40% were outside Southern Africa in a wide range of countries. The United Kingdom, the United States, Australia and Canada are primary destinations.
- Half of the migrants were sons and daughters or other relatives of household heads. However, the crisis in Zimbabwe is of such magnitude that household heads and spouses are migrating in significant numbers. Some 28% of the migrants were household heads and 13% were spouses/partners. More migrants were

married (58%) than unmarried (31%). All of this suggests a broadening and deepening of participation in labour migration.

- In most countries in SADC, migration still tends to be heavily male-dominated. Zimbabwe has become an exception to this rule. In this study 56% of migrants were male and 44% female.
- The majority of migrants (72%) are under the age of 40. They are also relatively well-educated compared to migrants from other SADC countries. Less than 1% have no schooling and over 50% have a post-secondary diploma, undergraduate degree or post-graduate degree.
- Migrants are employed in a wide variety of jobs outside Zimbabwe, many not in the profession for which they have training or skills. In other words, this is a generalized out-movement of people, not confined to one or two professions or sectors. Nineteen percent of migrants were in the informal sector, followed by professional work (15%), health (12%), services (9%), teaching (7%), manual work (6%) and office work (5%).
- Comparing in-country with out-of-country employment by sector, the survey showed that 70% of Zimbabwean health workers were migrants; as were over 40% of professional workers, service workers, managerial office workers and mineworkers. Between 30-40% of office workers and farm workers were also migrants. With teachers, the proportion was 28% and domestic workers 25%.
- Most migrants maintain close connections with Zimbabwe. Nearly half visit their families at least once every three months. However, almost 20% of the migrants (mostly living overseas) return home only once a year. Absences from home are highly variable: 18% are away for less than a month at a time, 19% between one and six months and 30% between six months and a year. Twenty percent are away for a year or longer.

The survey also provided unprecedented insights into the remittance behaviour of Zimbabwe's migrants, as well as invaluable information on the crucial importance of remittances to household survival. Although most migrant-sending households were struggling and poverty was increasing, very few could be considered destitute, at least on the evidence of this survey. However, without the constant and regular infusion of remittances from outside the country, the answers to this question would probably have been very different. Amongst the survey's key findings on remittances were the following:

- The vast majority of migrants regularly send back remittances in cash and/or kind. In the year prior to the study, three-quarters of migrant-sending households received remittances. Migrants sent home R2,759 p.a. on average. Various factors influenced the amounts remitted by individual migrants. For instance, heads of households remitted more than their children. Men remitted slightly more than women, an indication of greater labour market access in destination countries. Those in the 40-59 age group remitted more than migrants in any other age category. Furthermore, those who were married remitted more on average than those who were still single.

- Remittances come from a diverse range of countries and wide range of sectors. Migrants overseas remit more on average than those within Southern Africa. Within the region, the largest remitters are in Botswana followed by Zambia and South Africa.
- Professional workers, on average, send the most money back to Zimbabwe, followed by self-employed entrepreneurs, office workers and managers. Surprisingly, unskilled manual workers remit more, on average, than health workers, teachers, domestic workers and workers in the service sector.
- Most migrants remit on a regular basis. Some 61% of households receive money from migrants at least once a month. Another 25% receive money at least once or twice every three months and 7% once or twice a year. There was a positive correlation between the amount remitted and the frequency of remitting: migrants who send money home more frequently remit more on average than those who remit less often.
- Migrants use many different channels to send remittances home. In Zimbabwe, there is a clear preference for trusted informal channels over banks and formal money transfer operators such as Western Union and Moneygram. Social networks influence the channels through which informal remittances are sent. Active social ties between migrants and family members and friends provide the personal links and local information necessary for informal remittance sending.
- Decisions about how much will be remitted, how often and through what channels are not the sole preserve of the migrant. Households are in regular contact with their migrant members by phone and regularly send requests for emergency assistance. Eighty percent of households reported that migrants can be relied on to send emergency remittances most or all of the time.
- As many as 61% of the surveyed households had received goods in the year prior to the survey. Non-cash remittances included foodstuffs (for example, maize-meal, sugar, salt, and cooking oil) as well as consumer goods such as bicycles, radios, sofas, agricultural inputs and building materials. Most non-cash remitting is based on the specific and immediate needs of the recipients.

When the country faces shortages of basic commodities, non-cash remittances in the form of food tend to increase.

How important are remittances to household survival and sustainability in Zimbabwe? A broad distinction is often drawn between productive and consumptive uses of remittances. Since most remittances to Zimbabwe are aimed at easing the livelihood constraints of the households back home, consumption tends to dominate remittance usage. The survey's findings about remittance usage include:

- The vast majority of households receive cash and in-kind remittances. No other source of income came close in terms of the proportion of households that benefited. For example, despite the overall significance of informal sector trade only 15% of households generated income this way. A mere 6 % received income from the sale of farm products.
- Cash remittances were the major source of total household income, followed by wage work in Zimbabwe and remittance goods. The relative importance of remittances compared to other classes of income can be assessed via their importance to various basic household expenditure categories. Total expenses largely covered by remittances included gifts (93%), entertainment (92%), building (90%), clothes (88%), transportation (88%), education (88%), housing (85%), medical expenses (83%) and food and groceries (80%).
- The most common use of remittances is to buy food (by 67% of households), buy clothing (49%) and pay for school fees (48%). Domestic building materials are another common expense (by 49% of households) as are transportation costs (fuel and fares).
- The use of remittances to generate further income is not common although 27% of households used remittances to support food production and 12% purchased goods for re-sale. About 16% saved a portion of their remittances and 5% bought insurance policies. Nine percent spent remittances on funeral and burial policies and 8% on funerals – a clear indicator of the impact of HIV/AIDS.

The MARS study clearly shows that without remittance flows, the situation of many Zimbabwean households would be even more dire than it is already. Remittances have reduced vulnerability to hunger, ill-health and poverty in both rural and urban households. Households with migrants go without basic necessities less often. Remittances have also allowed families to keep children in school and to put roofs over the heads of household members. Remittances, as a major source of household income, clearly have an important impact on livelihoods in Zimbabwe.

INTRODUCTION

Migrant remittances, defined as transfers of funds and goods from migrants to relatives or friends in their country of origin, are now recognised as an important source of global development finance.[1] The economic impact of remittances has been considered beneficial at both micro and macro levels and there is increasing evidence that international remittances have considerable developmental impacts. Remittances provide much sought after foreign exchange to receiving countries. At the national level, remittances have a substantial effect on the balance of payments and on foreign exchange revenues while at the local level they supplement the earnings of millions of poor households. The contribution of remittances to GDP in many developing countries is significant and has shown a steady increase over the past decade.

While there is a consensus that remittance flows to Africa are increasing, little attention has been paid to the impact of these transfers on poverty alleviation, primarily because of data deficiencies at the household level.[2] Despite their obvious magnitude, accurate data on remittance flows to Zimbabwe is unavailable or inaccessible.[3] Data on remittances sent through formal channels is extremely difficult to obtain. In addition, massive flows of remittances through informal channels (particularly from neighbouring countries) go unrecorded. In an attempt to address these data deficiencies, SAMP devised the household-level Migration and Remittances Survey (MARS) which was administered in several SADC countries, including Zimbabwe.[4] The data generated by MARS is critical in at least three ways. Firstly, it quantifies the largely hidden economic value of labour migration from Zimbabwe. Second, it provides information on the significance of remittances to economic survival in a state undergoing massive formal sector and employment shrinkage. Third, it provides information on the relationship between remittances and poverty alleviation at the household level.

The MARS study was implemented in Zimbabwe in late 2004 and early 2005. Systematic sampling was used to randomly identify 723 migrant-sending households (HH). The sample was biased towards urban areas (77% of households) with 17% from rural areas and the remainder from peri-urban areas and small towns (Table 1). The two major cities in Zimbabwe – Harare and Bulawayo – were heavily sampled (25% and 12% of sampled households respectively). The relative under-sampling of rural households was because the survey coincided with the first half of the farming season and farmers were busy working in their fields. The political temperature in the countryside was also highly charged at this time. The households provided information on some 3,536 members, including over 800 migrants. This policy paper discusses the results of MARS in Zimbabwe, showing the major significance of remittances to household survival in a country in the midst of a major economic meltdown.

Table 1: Geographical Distribution of Respondents

District	Urban (Town/City)	Peri-Urban and Small Town	Rural	Total
Masvingo	59	-	7	66
Gweru	52	-	-	52
Kwekwe	38	-	1	39
Gokwe	-	1	7	8
Goromonzi	-	-	56	56
Nyanga	13	-	9	22
Chipinge	-	24	-	24
Harare	179	-	-	179
Seke/Chitungwiza	87	18	12	117
Mutare	30	-	-	30
Bulawayo	87	-	-	87
Insiza	-	-	25	25
Unknown	-	-	-	18
Total	545	43	117	723

PROFILE OF SAMPLE HOUSEHOLDS

As many as two-thirds of the household members captured by the survey were in economically-active age groups between 20 and 59 while only 4% were older than 60. There was an almost equal gender split in household membership (Table 2). The legacy of massive public investment in the education sector during the 1980s was clear: more than half of the household members had a primary or secondary education, 15% had diplomas while more than 10% had degrees and other post-graduate qualifications. Only 7% (mostly children under 10) had not received any formal education. Fifty one percent of household members were unmarried, 42% married, 4% widowed, and 2% divorced/separated/abandoned. Heads of households constituted 20% of the total household-member population, while spouses or partners made up 14%. Nearly 43% were children of the household head. Other household members included relatives such as brothers/sisters of the household head, grandchildren, nephews/nieces, sons/daughters-in-law, and parents and grandparents. Other relatives made up 3% and non-relatives just over 1% of the total household population.

Table 2: Profile of Household Members			
		No.	%
Sex	Male	1,746	49.4
	Female	1,786	50.6
N = 3532			
Age	0 – 9	375	11
	10-19	651	19.2
	20-29	1,024	30.1
	30-39	563	16.6
	40-49	372	11
	50-59	283	8.4
	60-69	103	3.1
	70+	25	0.7
N = 3396			
Marital Status	Unmarried	1,800	51
	Married	1,478	41.8
	Cohabiting	12	0.3
	Divorced/ Separated/ Abandoned	107	3.1
	Widowed	133	3.8
	Don't know	2	0.1
N = 3532			
Relationship to Head	Head	705	20.0
	Spouse/partner	496	14.1
	Son/ daughter	1,511	42.9
	Father/ mother	30	0.9
	Brother/ sister	294	8.3
	Grandchild	146	4.1
	Grandparent	21	0.6
	Son/ daughter-in-law	59	1.7
	Nephew/ niece	118	3.3
	Other relative	98	2.8
	Non-relative	46	1.3
N = 3524			
Education	None	232	6.7
	Primary/ Secondary	2,298	66.7
	Diploma	503	14.6
	Degree/ Postgraduate	363	10.6
	Don't know	47	1.4
N = 3443			

A considerable proportion of the households (44%) were nuclear in character (composed of a man and woman with or without children) (Table 3). Another 26% were extended (man and woman and children and relatives), 18% were female-centred (woman head with no partner/ spouse) and 9% were male-centred (male head with no partner/spouse). In the urban areas the number of nuclear households was double that of extended households, while in the rural areas the figures were almost equal.

Table 3: Household Type						
	Urban		Rural		Total	
	No.	%	No.	%	No.	%
Nuclear	263	37	48	7	311	44
Extended	134	19	46	7	180	26
Female-Centred	115	16	13	2	128	18
Male-Centred	58	8	8	1	66	9
Other	18	3	2	0	20	3
Total	588	83	117	17	705	100

Extended households typically consist of a husband, wife, several children and grandparents and grandchildren. Grandparents and grandchildren were more numerous in the rural households surveyed. The dependency ratio is therefore higher in the economically under-performing rural areas. Migration of young adults and HIV/AIDS-related deaths have robbed many young children of their parents.[5] Although child-headed households are becoming more common, most affected children end up staying with close relatives, such as aunts, uncles or grandparents. In households where one or both parents have left the country a 'new spatially-stretched' family unit has emerged characterized by multiple earning sources at various geographical localities.[6]

The occupational categories of the household members varied but were dominated by two economically unproductive groups – "scholar/ students" and "unemployed/job seekers." Together, these two groups constituted 36% of the total household population (Table 4). Nine percent were in informal sector activities such as trading and vending. Of the total of 1,382 household members in paid employment, 18% were professionals, 14% teachers, 11% service workers, 10% health workers, 8% office workers and 8% self-employed entrepreneurs. Skilled and unskilled manual workers made up only 7% of the employed, a clear reflection of high unemployment rates in the country. Other jobs held by household members included domestic work, office work, minework, farmwork and police/military/security work.

Table 4: Main Occupations of Household Members		
	No. of HH Members	% of Total Members
Occupations Scholar/ Student	865	25.0
Unemployed/ Job seeker	389	11.3
Trader/ hawker/ vendor/ Informal sector producer	302	8.7
Professional worker	247	7.1
Too young to work	202	5.8
Teacher	199	5.8
Service worker	153	4.4
Health worker	133	3.8
Office worker	116	3.4
Businessman/ woman (self-employed)	112	3.2
House work (unpaid)	109	3.2
Skilled/unskilled manual worker	100	2.9
Domestic worker	74	2.1
Pensioner	71	2.1
Managerial office worker	67	1.9
Don't know	59	1.7
Mine worker	58	1.7
Farmer	44	1.3
Police/ Military/ Security personnel	35	1.0
Agricultural worker	28	0.8
Employer/ Manager	16	0.5
Foreman	15	0.4
Other	61	1.8
Totals	3455	99.9

Obtaining accurate data on household income is a major research challenge. Most households do not keep records of money earned from various sources, particularly from informal jobs and remittances.[7] The research therefore had to rely on estimates provided by respondents, and as a result should be treated as indicative rather than definitive. The average total reported household income for the sample was the equivalent of R7,415 per annum (Table 5). However, between 70-80% of households earned less than the mean with over 20% earning less than R1,000 per month.

Table 5: Total Household Income from All Sources	
Percentile	Rand
10th	501
20th	911
30th	1,457
40th	2,186
50th	3,142
60th	4,102
70th	5,410
80th	7,651
90th	12,660
Mean	7,416
N = 581	

The harsh economic climate compels many households to borrow money to take care of their monthly bills. Just over a third of surveyed households had borrowed money in the previous year from friends and family (Table 6). Only a handful (6.5%) borrowed from banks and even fewer from formal or informal money lenders (3% and 1% respectively). This suggests a healthy suspicion of all forms of usury. Reciprocity is more likely to be the operating principle, as loans from friends and family are unlikely to carry significant interest charges. Most borrowing was to meet pressing needs including food (about 12% of households), school fees (10%), travel and funeral expenses, and medical costs.

Table 6: Sources of Borrowed Funds		
	No. of HH	% of Total HH
Friends	167	23.7
Family	85	12.1
Bank	46	6.5
Employer	28	4.0
Money lenders (formal)	23	3.3
Church	11	1.6
Money lenders (informal)	10	1.4
Micro-finance organisations	5	0.7
Burial society	3	0.4
Other sources	1	0.1
N=705		

The majority of household income is spent on basic necessities. The highest mean expenditures in the month preceding the survey were on building (R604), medical expenses (R464), farming (R169), education

(R131) and food (R107) (Table 7). However, the number of households that spent money on building and farming was small (at 11.5% and 6.5% respectively). Many more households incurred expenses for food (89%), education (57%) and medical attention (38%). The overall importance of these three expenditure categories is emphasized by the weighted values for monthly expenditure (Table 6).[8] Food and groceries were clearly the most important item (total spend for all households of R40,040), followed by education (R18,171), clothing (R16,167) and building (R14,755). Total expenditures on farming were slight (R3,352), even less than on gifts and entertainment. While 16% of the sampled households were rural, only 6.5% spent money on farming.

Table 7: Monthly Household Expenses				
Spending Category:	No. of HH	Mean (R)	Median (R)	Weighted Value for All Households (R)
Food and groceries	628	107	64	40,040
Housing	318	28	9	2,896
Utilities	477	29	10	4,649
Clothes	355	87	46	16,167
Alcohol	108	27	18	1,967
Medical expenses	271	464	18	4,937
Transportation	328	75	23	7,467
Cigarettes, tobacco, snuff	20	13	6	128
Education	399	131	46	18,171
Entertainment	67	24	9	610
Fuel	36	12	5	164
Farming	46	169	73	3,352
Building	81	604	182	14,755
Special events	85	83	27	2,323
Gifts	28	106	23	638
Other expenses	8	945	20	164
N = 705				

Poor households in the rural and urban areas of Zimbabwe are engaged in a grinding struggle for survival and most household income is used for basic food items. On average, households spend as much as a third of their income on food. The percentage of income devoted to food expenditures can be used as a basic poverty indicator to further differentiate between households in the sample. Forty-two percent of households said they spend 40% or more of their income on food (Table 8). Twelve percent spend over 70% of their income on food and can be considered extremely poor.

Table 8: Food Poverty Index			
% of HH Expenditure Devoted to Food (FPI)	No. of HH	% of HH	Cumulative %
10-19	63	12	12
20-29	121	21	33
30-39	144	25	58
40-49	86	15	73
50-59	58	10	83
60-69	29	5	88
70-79	35	5	93
80-89	23	4	97
90+	16	3	100
N = 575			

The Lived Poverty Index (LPI) is another measure of the extent and distribution of household poverty.[9] Respondents were asked how often they went without some of the basic necessities of life (including food to eat, clean water, medical attention, electricity, fuel and a cash income) in the previous year. The LPI scale runs from 0 (complete satisfaction of basic needs) to 4 (frequent shortages of basic needs). While 69% of households said they had never gone without enough food in the previous year, 29% had gone without several times, and 2% said they never had enough food to eat (Table 9). With regard to clean water and cooking fuel, again the majority (around three-quarters) had never gone without. Less than 1% of households were always without these commodities. Despite Zimbabwe's medical brain drain, 74% of respondents said their household had never gone without medical treatment or medicine. Only 55% had never gone without a cash income.

Although most households were struggling and poverty was increasing, very few could be considered destitute, at least on the evidence of this survey. The clue to resolving the puzzle is remittances. In other words, without the constant and regular infusion of remittances from outside the country, the answers to this question would probably have been very different. This is confirmed by a comparison with a national survey of Zimbabwe households by the Afrobarometer project.[10] The LPI score for the MARS households was 0.44 compared with a national score of 1.74.[11]

Table 9: Lived Poverty Index		No.	%	Mean LPI
Not Had Enough Food	Never	500	69.2	0.17
	Just once or twice	151	20.9	0.77
	Several times	57	7.9	1.45
	Many times	13	1.8	1.91
	Always	2	0.3	2.30
N = 723				
Not Had Enough Clean Water for Home Use	Never	561	77.6	0.23
	Just once or twice	103	14.2	0.91
	Several times	34	4.7	1.27
	Many times	23	3.2	1.94
	Always	2	0.3	2.70
N = 723				
Gone Without Medicine or Medical Treatment?	Never	529	73.9	0.19
	Just once or twice	131	18.3	0.85
	Several times	44	6.1	1.51
	Many times	9	1.3	2.47
	Always	2	0.3	2.40
N = 716				
Not Had Enough Fuel to Cook Food	Never	536	77.1	0.22
	Just once or twice	97	14.0	0.86
	Several times	43	6.2	1.44
	Many times	12	1.7	1.78
	Always	7	1.0	2.44
N = 695				
Gone Without A Cash Income?	Never	395	54.8	0.09
	Just once or twice	187	25.9	0.59
	Several times	98	13.6	1.00
	Many times	29	4.0	1.68
	Always	12	1.7	1.90
N = 721				

CROSS-BORDER MIGRATION

I s the heavy dependence of Zimbabwean households on remittances actually something new in Zimbabwe? Migrants have been leaving the country for work and remitting for many decades. For example, 29% of the respondents had parents and 10% had grand-parents who had worked outside Zimbabwe. In both cases, migrants had gone to work in neighbouring countries, primarily South Africa (Table 10). Thirteen percent of the grandparents had worked in non-SADC countries, compared to 20% of parents. These figures tend to suggest that migration increases in volume and becomes more diverse in destination as we move closer to the present.

Table 10: Country of Migration of Parents and Grandparents				
	Parents		Grandparents	
	No.	%	No.	%
South Africa	91	44.0	40	54.1
Mozambique	20	9.7	8	10.8
Botswana	16	7.7	3	4.1
Malawi	14	6.8	8	10.8
Zambia	14	6.8	2	2.7
Namibia	4	1.9	1	1.4
Angola	2	1.0	2	2.7
Lesotho	2	1.0	-	-
Swaziland	2	1.0	-	-
Tanzania	1	0.5	-	-
Other country	41	19.8	10	13.5
Total	207	100.0	74	100.0
N=705				

The recent dramatic increase in migration from Zimbabwe was confirmed by the survey.[12] Most of the migrants (72%) had worked outside the country for 5 years or less. Only 7% had been working for over 10 years as migrants, although one man had worked for 40 years (Table 11).

Nearly one-third of the household members in the survey were cross-border migrants. The number of migrants per household varied from one to five. The majority (73%) had a single migrant, and another 21% had two (Table 12). In other words, many households rely very heavily on one or two migrants.

Table 11: Period Worked as Migrant		
Years	No.	%
1 – 5	611	71.6
6 – 10	177	20.8
11 – 15	38	4.5
26 – 20	14	1.6
19 – 25	7	0.8
26 – 30	1	0.1
31 or more	2	0.2
Don't know	3	0.4
Total	853	100.0

Table 12: Number of Migrants per Household		
No. of Migrants	No. of HH	%
1	513	72.8
2	147	20.9
3	38	5.4
4	6	0.9
5	1	0.1
Total	705	100.0

The survey found that 58% of migrants were in neighbouring countries, primarily South Africa (32%), Botswana (16%) and Mozambique (5%) (Table 13).

Table 13: Destination Country of Migrants		
	No.	%
South Africa	260	32.3
Mozambique	41	5.1
Namibia	10	1.2
Botswana	130	16.1
Malawi	7	0.9
Zambia	17	2.1
Tanzania	2	0.2
Other	338	42.0
Total	805	100.0

The other 42% were outside Southern Africa in a wide range of countries. These were not identified by name in the survey. However, data from the OECD shows the dominance of the United Kingdom, the United States, Australia and Canada as destinations (Table 14). Many European countries had several hundred Zimbabweans living there.

Table 14: Non-African Zimbabwean Migrant Destinations		
Destination	No.	%
United Kingdom	49,524	57.2
Australia	11,734	13.6
United States	11,740	13.6
Canada	4,185	0.48
New Zealand	2,886	0.33
Ireland	1,462	0.17
Portugal	1,352	0.16
Netherlands	1,018	0.12
Switzerland	522	0.6
Greece	448	0.5
France	350	0.4
Sweden	320	0.4
Belgium	318	0.4
Other	695	0.8
Total	86,554	88.8
Source: OECD		

Half of the migrants were sons and daughters or other relatives of household heads. This is the classic historical pattern of labour migration from Zimbabwe and within Southern Africa more generally. However, the crisis in Zimbabwe is of such magnitude that household heads and spouses are now also migrating in significant numbers. In this study, 28% of the migrants were household heads and 13% were spouses/partners (Table 15). More migrants are currently married (58%) versus 31% unmarried which, again, is a switch from the classic pattern, suggesting a broadening and deepening of participation in labour migration. In most countries in SADC, migration still tends to be heavily male-dominated. Zimbabwe has become an exception to this rule. In this study 56% of migrants were male and 44% female.

The majority of migrants (72%) are under the age of 40 with most of those (56%) in the 25 to 39 age group. In other words, migrants are generally individuals in their prime working years. They are also relatively well-educated compared to migrants from other SADC countries. Less than 1% have no schooling and over 50% have a post-secondary diploma, undergraduate degree or post-graduate degree.

Table 15: Demographic Profile of Migrants		No.	%
Relationship	Head	226	28.3
	Spouse/ Partner	101	12.6
	Son/ Daughter	286	35.8
	Father/ Mother	7	0.9
	Brother/ Sister	115	14.4
	Grandchild	2	0.3
	Son/ Daughter-in-law	8	1.0
	Nephew/ Niece	18	2.3
	Other relative	30	3.8
	Non-relative	7	0.9
Total		800	100.0
Sex	Male	450	55.9
	Female	355	44.1
Total		805	100.0
Age	15 to 24	124	15.4
	25 to 39	454	56.4
	40 to 59	185	23.0
	60 and over	7	0.9
	Don't know	35	4.3
Total		805	100.0
Marital status	Unmarried	247	30.7
	Married	469	58.3
	Cohabiting	7	0.9
	Divorced/ Separated/ Abandoned	45	5.6
	Widowed	37	4.6
Total		805	100.0
Education	None	6	0.8
	Primary/ Secondary	383	47.9
	Diploma	225	28.1
	Degree/ Postgraduate	182	22.8
	Don't know	4	0.5
Total		800	100.0

The survey showed that migrants are employed in a wide variety of jobs outside Zimbabwe. In other words, this is a generalized out-movement of people, not confined to one or two professions or sectors. Nineteen percent of migrants were in the informal sector, followed by professional work (15%), health (12%), services (9%), teaching (7%), manual work (6%) and office work (5%) (Table 15). Comparing in-country with out-of-country employment by sector, the survey showed that 70% of health workers were migrants (Table 16). Over 40% of professional workers, service workers, managerial office workers and mineworkers were migrants. Between 30-40% of office workers and farm workers were also migrants outside the country. With teachers, the proportion was 28% and domestic workers 25%. Only in the security and military sector and in farming were there significantly more people employed inside the country than out of it.

Table 16: Migrant Occupations			
Occupation	Total No. in Job/Sector	No. of Migrants	% Migrants
Scholar/ Student	865	10	1.1
Trader/ hawker/ vendor/ Informal sector producer	302	154	51.0
Professional worker	247	120	48.6
Teacher	199	56	28.1
Service worker	153	72	47.1
Health worker	133	92	69.2
Office worker	116	40	34.5
Businessman/ woman (self-employed)	112	33	29.5
Skilled/unskilled manual worker	100	50	50.0
Domestic worker	74	18	24.3
Managerial office worker	67	29	43.3
Mine worker	58	24	41.4
Farmer	44	5	11.4
Police/ Military/ Security personnel	35	5	14.3
Agricultural worker	28	11	39.3
Employer/ Manager	16	10	62.5
Foreman	15	6	40.0
Other	61	23	37.7
Total	2625	758	34.6

Most migrants maintain close connections with Zimbabwe. Nearly half visit their families at least once every three months. However, almost 20% of the migrants (mostly living overseas) return home only once a year (Table 17). Absences from home are highly variable: 18% are away for less than a month at a time, 19% between one and six months and 30% between six months and a year. Twenty percent are away for a year or longer. Social networks are extremely important in determining where migrants stay while away: only a quarter stay alone. The rest stay with other household members 18%), friends (16.5%), relatives (15%) or co-workers from Zimbabwe (13%).

Table 17: Return Migration		No.	%
Frequency of Return	Twice or more per month	138	16.5
	Once a month	121	14.5
	More than twice in 3 months	65	7.8
	Once in 3 months	90	10.8
	Once every 6 months	57	6.8
	Once a year	159	19.0
	At end of the contract	33	3.9
	Other	173	20.7
Total		836	100.0
Time Away	Less than one month	152	18.3
	More than one month but less than six months	154	18.6
	More than six months but less than one year	245	29.6
	One year at a time	59	7.1
	Longer than 1 year at a time	110	13.3
	Other	109	13.1
Total		829	100.0
Residence at Destination	Alone	201	24.1
	With another household member	149	17.9
	With another relative	122	14.6
	With a friend	138	16.5
	With co-worker/s	110	13.2
	Other	41	4.9
	Don't know	73	8.8
Total		834	100.0

Other SAMP studies have shown that the emigration potential of people in Zimbabwe is extraordinarily high.[13] While remittances may exercise a dampening effect on migration, they are certainly not sufficient to discourage it altogether. For example, around 20% of adult household members in the MARS survey were planning to go and work in another country in the upcoming year. Most were likely to go to neighbouring countries, reproducing existing migration streams. Countries cited most often were South Africa (36.5%), Botswana (11.5%) and Namibia (2.7%) (Table 18). Forty-four percent wanted to leave the region. The continued emigration of skilled workers was also confirmed. Health workers made up 14% of intending migrants, professional workers (11%), teachers (7%), and office workers and service workers (5%).

Table 18: Most Likely Destination

	No.	%
South Africa	149	36.5
Botswana	47	11.5
Namibia	11	2.7
Mozambique	9	2.2
Malawi	4	1.0
Zambia	4	1.0
Zimbabwe	2	0.5
Angola	1	0.2
Lesotho	1	0.2
Swaziland	1	0.2
Tanzania	1	0.2
Other	178	43.6
Total	408	100.0

MIGRATION AND REMITTANCES

Surveyed households saw migration as playing a crucial livelihoods role: over 90% said that migrancy had a positive or very positive effect and less than 1% saw the effect as negative or very negative. Nearly 90% regarded remittances as important for household food security and 76% in providing money for medicine or medical treatment (Table 19).

Table 19: Perceived Importance of Remittances to Household

	Important		Neutral		Unimportant	
	No.	%	No.	%	No.	%
Enough food to eat?	586	88.5	51	7.7	25	3.8
Enough clean water for home use?	389	59.8	147	22.6	115	17.7
Medicine or medical treatment?	491	75.9	89	13.8	67	10.4
Electricity in your home	414	64.5	120	18.7	108	16.8
Enough fuel to cook your food?	359	57.2	150	23.9	119	18.9
N= 653						

The vast majority of migrants regularly send back remittances in cash and/or kind. Indeed, the figure is so high that earning money to remit is clearly a major motivator for migration in the first place. In the year prior to the study, for example, three-quarters of migrant-sending households received remittances. Migrants sent home R2,759 per annum on average. Various factors influence the amounts remitted by individual migrants. For instance, heads of households remitted more cash (R3,726) than their children (R2,311). Men (R2,872) remitted slightly more than women (R2,612) – an indication of greater labour market access in destination countries. Those in the 40-59 age group remitted more cash on average (R5,365) than migrants in any other age category. Furthermore, those who were married remitted more on average (R3,176) than those who were still single (R1,924).

Remittances come from a diverse range of countries and wide range of sectors. Migrants overseas remit more on average than those within Southern Africa. Within the region, the largest remitters are in Botswana followed by Zambia and South Africa (Table 20).

Table 20: Annual Cash Remittances by Place of Work		
Current Place of Work	No.	Mean (R)
South Africa	245	1,808
Mozambique	38	1,565
Namibia	10	1,600
Botswana	120	3,433
Malawi	7	1,744
Zambia	16	1,877
Tanzania	1	674
Other	313	3,503

Professional workers, on average, send the most money back to Zimbabwe, followed by self-employed entrepreneurs, office workers and managers (Table 21). Surprisingly, unskilled manual workers remit more, on average, than health workers, teachers, domestic workers and workers in the service sector.

Most migrants send money home on a regular basis. In the survey, 61% of households said they receive money from migrants at least once a month (Table 22). Another 25% receive money at least once or twice every three months and 7% once or twice a year. There was a positive correlation between the amount remitted and the frequency of remitting (Table 23). Migrants who send money home more frequently remit more on average than those who remit less often. Those who remit twice or more a year, for example, send back an average R3,716 compared with R1,239 from those who remit only once a year.

Table 21: Annual Cash Remittances by Profession

Main Occupation	Mean (R)	Minimum (R)	Maximum (R)
Farmer	702	7	1,822
Agricultural worker (paid)	1,376	109	3,188
Agricultural worker (unpaid)	9	9	9
Service worker	1,187	18	5,465
Domestic worker	1,663	109	7,651
Managerial office worker	3,166	9	17,943
Office worker	3,598	36	72,866
Foreman	1,591	73	4,554
Mine worker	1,598	109	5,465
Skilled manual worker	1,952	18	7,287
Unskilled manual worker	2,472	18	10,930
Informal sector producer	2,219	73	18,216
Trader/ hawker/ vendor	1,703	4	63,758
Security personnel	209	55	364
Police/ Military	1,275	455	2,732
Businessman/ woman (self-employed)	4,136	9	35,522
Employer/ Manager	3,387	546	6,831
Professional worker	6,043	0.5	91,082
Teacher	1,728	5	10,930
Health worker	2,369	36	9,108
Scholar/ Student	1,740	137	5,465
Other	1,766	91	9,108
Total	2,723	0.5	91,082

Table 22: Frequency of Remitting by Destination

Frequency	SADC Countries		Other		Total	
	No.	%	No.	%	No.	%
Twice or more per month	53	52.5	48	47.5	101	12.8
Once a month	231	60.9	148	39.1	379	48.2
More than twice in 3 months	49	9.0	22	31.0	71	9.0
Once in three months	71	55.0	58	45.0	129	16.4
Once every 6 months	21	60.0	14	40.0	35	4.4
Once a year	9	42.9	12	57.1	21	2.7
At end of the contract	1	50	1	50.0	2	0.3
Other	15	50	15	50.0	30	3.8
Don't know	9	47.4	10	52.6	19	2.4
Total	459	58.3	328	41.7	787	100.0

Table 23: Annual Remittances by Frequency of Remitting		
	No.	Mean (R)
Twice or more per month	97	3,717
Once a month	370	3,253
More than twice in 3 months	66	2,208
Once in three months	122	1,563
Once every 6 months	34	1,488
Once a year	19	1,236
At end of the contract	2	683
Other	30	2,409
Don't know	10	2,130
N= 760		

The amount of money personally brought by migrants on their last visit home also varied although very few (5%) came home empty-handed. The majority (60%) brought home less than R91 (Table 24).

Table 24: Value of Money Brought Home on Last Visit		
Value in Z$	No.	%
None	25	5.0
1 – 1,000,000 (R1-91)	299	60.2
1,000,001- 2,000,000 (R92-182)	27	5.4
2,000,001- 3,000,000 (R183-273)	28	5.6
3,000,001- 4,000,000 (R274-364)	8	1.6
4,000,001-5,000,000 (R365-455)	7	1.4
5,000,001- 6,000,000 (R456-546)	5	1.0
> 6,000,000 (>R547)	42	8.5
Total	441	100.0

Migrants use many different channels to send remittances home. There is a basic distinction between formal channels (including money transfer services by banks and non-bank financial institutions such as foreign exchange bureaus or dedicated money transfer operators) and informal channels (which include the hand carrying of cash by migrants or their family and friends, as well as transfers through unregulated money transfer operators). In Zimbabwe, there is a clear preference for trusted informal channels over banks or formal money transfer operators such as Western Union and Moneygram. Social networks influence the channels through which informal remittances are sent. Active social ties between migrants and family members and friends provide the personal links and local information necessary for informal remittance sending.

Almost half of the households reported that migrants either bring cash with them when they return home to visit the family (35%) or send remittances via friends and co-workers (11%). Another informal, less reliable, method used by a few is transport by taxi-drivers. In terms of formal channels, around a quarter (26%) said they send funds via a bank in Zimbabwe and 14.5% through the Post Office (Table 25).

Table 25: Main Methods of Cash Remitting Used by Migrants		
Method of Transfer	No.	%
Brings personally	320	34.6
Via Bank in Home Country	237	25.6
Via Post Office	134	14.5
Via Friend/Co-Worker	102	11
Via Taxis	26	2.8
Bank in South Africa	12	1.3
Bus	1	0.1
Other method	91	9.8
Don't know	2	0.2
Total	923	100.0

Focus group discussions indicated that there had been a shift towards greater use of formal channels due, firstly, to a wider network of money transfer agencies and, second, to an extensive media blitz by the Reserve Bank of Zimbabwe directed to encouraging Zimbabweans out of the country to shift to formal channels. With the collapse of Homelink and the Zimbabwean dollar, informal channels have become more significant again.

The problems experienced in money transfers varied with the type of method used. Excessive charges were associated with the use of banks and the Post Office (Table 26). On the other hand, sending the money via a friend or a co-worker was often seen as being slow and unreliable and more likely to be lost or stolen. Bringing the money home personally was more reliable but theft was also a problem and there could be long delays for the household unless the migrant travelled home regularly.

Decisions about how much to remit, how often and through what channels are not the sole preserve of the migrant. Households said they are in regular contact with their migrant members by phone and regularly send requests for emergency assistance. A number of problems are experienced by the household in contacting the migrant whenever they require assistance. At times the migrant might not have the resources to send when they contact him or her. Problems and delays are also experienced in contacting the migrant. Other problems experienced include slow transport and limited financial and banking services. Nevertheless, 80%

of the households reported that migrants can be relied on to send emergency remittances most or all of the time. Only 3% said they can rarely, if ever, rely on receiving remittances from their migrants.

Table 26: Problems Experienced by Method Used

	Costly charges		Slow		Unreliable		Lack of banking facilities		Irregular		Never arrives, gets stolen		Other problem		Don't know		Total	
	No.	%	No	%	No	%	No	%	No	%	No	%	No	%	No	%	No	%
Via bank in home country	58	31.0	19	25.0	12	15.6	6	40.0	2	14.3	7	11.7	5	41.7	0	0.0	109	24.7
Via the Post Office	53	28.3	17	22.4	7	9.1	3	20.0	4	28.6	6	10.0	1	8.3	0	0.0	91	20.6
Brings it along	41	21.9	18	23.7	19	24.7	5	33.3	6	42.9	29	48.3	2	16.7	1	100	121	27.4
Via a friend/co-worker	9	4.8	15	19.7	20	26	0	0.0	2	14.3	18	30.0	0	0.0	0	0.0	64	14.5
Via Taxis	7	3.7	2	2.6	4	5.2	1	6.7	0	0.0	0	0.0	0	0.0	0	0.0	14	3.2
Bank in South Africa	3	1.6	4	5.3	2	2.6	0	0.0	0	0.0	0	0.0	0	0.0	0	0.0	9	2.0
Other method	16	8.6	1	1.3	13	16.9	0	0.0	0	0.0	0	0.0	4	33.3	0	0.0	34	7.7
Total	187	100	76	100	77	100	15	100	14	100	60	100	12	100	1	100	442	100

REMITTING IN KIND

While remittances are generally seen as involving cash transfers, in Southern African it is important to consider goods purchased and sent home by migrants as a form of remittance. As many as 61% of the surveyed households reported that they had received goods from their migrant members in the year prior to the survey. Non-cash remittances included foodstuffs (for example, maize-meal, sugar, salt, and cooking oil) as well as consumer goods such as bicycles, radios, sofas, agricultural inputs and building materials. Most non-cash remitting is based on the specific and immediate needs of the recipients. When the country faces shortages of basic commodities, non-cash remittances in the form of food tend to increase.

Most goods are brought by the migrants themselves (60%) when they come home to visit (Table 27). Some send goods via mail (12%) or with a friend or co-worker (10%). Very few use public transportation services such as buses (only 5%) or rail (1%). Some had complaints about costly charges, slowness and theft but the problems appear less significant than with cash transfers.

Table 27: Preferred Method of Remitting Goods

Preferred Method	No.	%
Official transport – Bus	40	5.3
Official transport – Rail	8	1.1
Via Post Office	89	11.9
Sends with a taxi	11	1.5
Brings personally	454	60.5
Via a friend/ co-worker	78	10.4
Sends with visiting family members	30	4.0
Other	40	5.3
Total	830	100.0

As with cash, most migrants come home bearing goods of some kind. In most cases, the value of the goods brought home was under R182 (69%) although a few brought goods valued at over R546 (Table 28).

Table 28: Value of Goods Brought Home

Value in Z$	No.	%
None	32	6.7
1 – 1,000,000 (R1-91)	80	16.8
1,000,001- 2,000,000 (R92-182)	249	52.3
2,000,001- 3,000,000 (R183-273)	8	1.7
3,000,001- 4,000,000 (R274-364)	5	1.1
4,000,001-5,000,000 (R365-455)	7	1.5
5,000,001- 6,000,000 (R456-546)	1	0.2
> 6,000,000 (>R547)	33	6.9
Don't know	49	10.3
No Answer	12	2.5
Total	476	100.0

REMITTANCES AND LIVELIHOODS

How important are remittances to household survival and sustainability in Zimbabwe? A broad distinction is often drawn in the literature between productive and consumptive uses of remittances.[14] Since most remittances to Zimbabwe are aimed at easing the livelihood constraints of the households back home, consumption tends to dominate remittance usage. The more immediate needs of the families are usually food, housing, education and healthcare. These can be seen as important "investments" in human capital terms.

Firstly, the vast majority of surveyed households received cash and in-kind remittances. No other source of income came close in terms of the proportion of households that benefited. For example, despite the overall significance of informal sector trade only 15% of households generated income this way. A mere 6 % received income from the sale of farm products.

Second, there is the question of what proportion of household income in migrant-sending households comes from remittances. The survey suggested that average income earned from formal business (R5,738 per household), informal business (R4,463) and wage work (R3,917) were more important than remittances in either cash (R2,641) or goods (R1,275) (Table 29). However, when the weighted value of total household income sources is calculated, cash remittances were the major source of total household income (R597,865) followed by wage work (R465,613), and remittance goods (R197,193).

Table 29: Household Income					
Source of Income	No. of Households Receiving Income from Source	% of Households Receiving Income from Source	Mean Annual Household Income from Source (R)	Median Annual Household Income from Source (R)	Weighted Total Income of All Households (R)
Wage work	355	43.3	3,898	1,312	465,613
Casual work	65	9.2	1,404	364	23,681
Remittances – money	547	77.6	2,672	1,093	597,865
Remittances – goods	433	61.4	1,239	455	197,193
Income from farm products	45	6.4	970	228	10,292
Income from formal business	62	8.8	5,748	137	8,471
Income from informal business	105	14.9	4,477	638	66,946
Pension/disability	48	6.8	857	223	10,748
Gifts	35	5.0	345	91	3,188
Other income	6	0.5	15,377	20,038	120,229
Note: More than one answer permitted					

Third, the relative importance of remittances compared to other classes of income can be assessed via their contribution to various basic household expenditure categories. Expenses largely covered by remittances included gifts (93% from remittances), entertainment (92%), building (90%), clothes (88%), transportation (88%), education (88%), housing (85%), medical expenses (83%) and food and groceries (80%) (Figure 1).

Figure 1: Average Share of Expenses Paid from Remittances

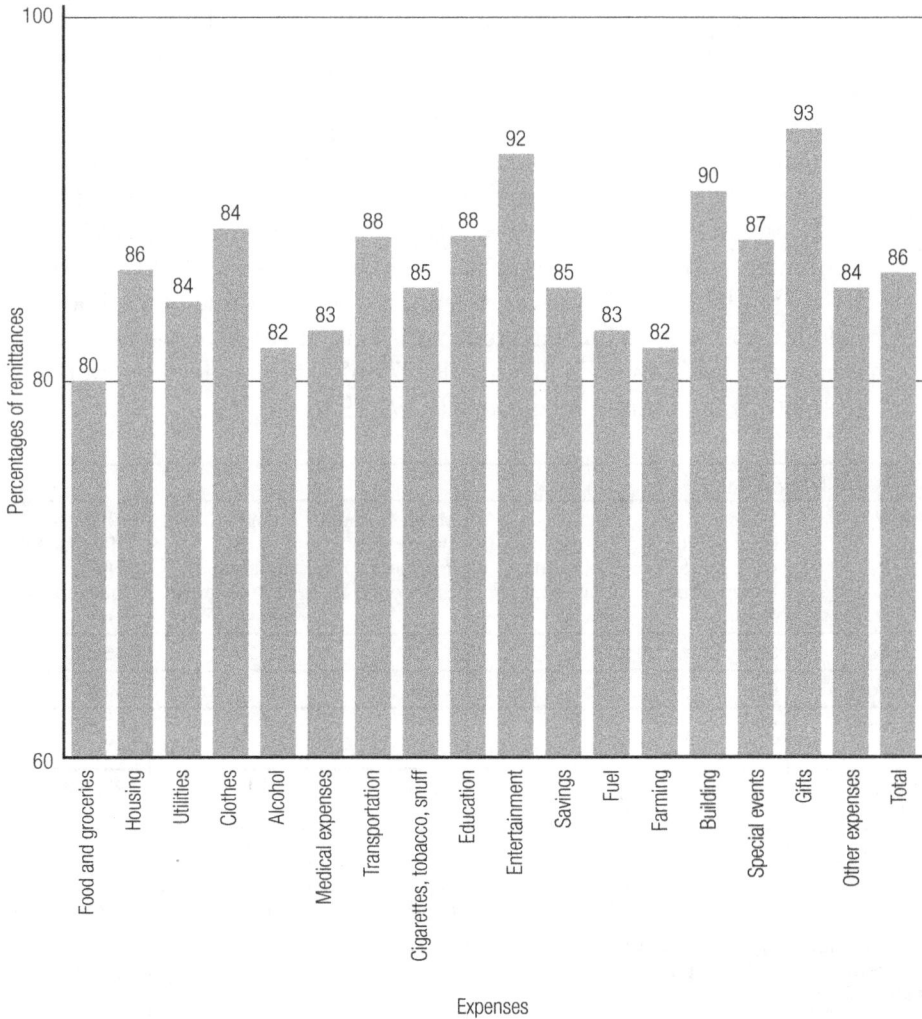

Fourth, households perceive migrant remittances as vital to many of their livelihood needs. Remittances were seen as very important (by over 80% of respondents) to the purchase of building materials (89%), school fees (84%), vehicle purchase (84%), buying machinery (83%), food (81%) and fuel (81%) (Table 30).

Table 30: Perceived Importance of Remittances to Household Expenditures

	Very Important		Important		Neutral		Not Important		Not Important at All		Total	
	No	%	No	%	No	%	No	%	No	%	No	%
School fees	268	84.3	39	12.3	9	2.8	2	0.6	0	.0	318	100.0
Food	336	81.4	61	14.8	15	3.6	1	0.2	0	.0	413	100.0
Clothing	160	54.8	90	30.8	40	13.7	2	0.7	0	.0	292	100.0
Vehicle and transport costs	6	50.0	4	33.3	2	16.7	-	-	-	-	12	100.0
Equipment	2	28.6	5	71.4	-	-	-	-	-	-	7	100.0
Farming activities	97	62.2	44	28.2	15	9.6	-	-	-	-	156	100.0
Fares	105	67.3	31	19.9	18	11.5	2	1.3	-	-	156	100.0
Fuel	30	81.1	4	10.8	2	5.4	-	-	1	2.7	37	100.0
Vehicle purchase and mainte-nance	36	83.7	5	11.6	2	4.7	-	-	-	-	43	100.0
Other transport expenses	1	100.0	-	-	-	-	-	-	-	-	1	100.0
Purchase goods for sale (stock)	51	71.8	18	25.4	1	1.4	1	1.4	-	-	71	100.0
Repay loans	9	56.3	7	43.8	-	-	-	-	-	-	16	100.0
Machinery and equipment	10	83.3	2	16.7	-	-	-	-	-	-	12	100.0
Other business expenses	5	71.4	1	14.3	1	14.3	-	-	-	-	7	100.0
Building Materials	108	89.3	8	6.6	3	2.5	-	0.0	2	1.7	121	100.0
Insurance policies	13	65.0	3	15.0	3	15.0	1	5.0	-	-	20	100.0
Funeral and burial policies	29	65.9	9	20.5	4	9.1	2	4.5	-	-	44	100.0
Other personal investment	9	69.2	2	15.4	1	7.7	1	7.7	-	-	13	100.0
Marriage	4	44.4	5	55.6	-	-	-	-	-	-	9	100.0
Funeral	33	75.0	10	22.7	1	2.3	-	-	-	-	44	100.0
Feast	6	60.0	1	10.0	3	30.0	-	-	-	-	10	100.0
Other spe-cial events	1	100.0	-	-	-	-	-	-	-	-	1	100.0
Other expenditure items	10	90.9	1	9.1	-	-	-	-	-	-	11	100.0

Finally, the most pervasive use of remittances is to buy food (by 67% of households averaging R938 per household), clothing (by 49% of households averaging R455 per household) and pay for school fees (by 48% averaging R492) (Table 31). Domestic building materials are another common expense (by 49% of households averaging R738 per household) as are transportation costs (fuel and fares). The use of remittances to generate further income is not common although 27% of households used remittances to support food production and 12% purchased goods for re-sale. About 16% saved a portion of their remittances and 5% bought insurance policies. Nine percent spent remittances on funeral and burial policies and 8% on funerals – a clear indicator of the impact of HIV/AIDS.

Table 31: Expenditure of Remittances			
	No. of HH	% of HH	Average Amount Spent (R)
School fees	342	48.5	493
Food	472	67.0	936
Clothing	346	49.1	459
Vehicle and transport costs	14	2.0	272
Equipment	10	1.4	726
Farming activities	189	26.8	530
Fares	205	29.1	319
Fuel	47	6.7	480
Vehicle purchase and maintenance	50	7.1	2,053
Other transport expenses	1	0.1	46
Purchase goods for sale (stock)	87	12.3	2,114
Repay loans	22	3.1	793
Labour costs	20	2.8	437
Machinery and equipment	14	2.0	1,171
Other business expenses	10	1.4	467
Building materials	349	49.5	740
Savings	114	16.2	1,698
Insurance policies	33	4.7	2,393
Funeral and burial policies	61	8.7	347
Other personal investment	11	1.6	1,356
Marriage	13	1.8	211
Funeral	55	7.8	119
Feast	13	1.8	88
Other special events	3	0.3	2,991

Despite the livelihoods pressures on remittances, many households did use them to purchase consumer goods. A wide range of consumer items had been acquired through remittances (Table 32).

Table 32: Goods Remitted or Purchased with Cash Remittances		
	No. of HH with Item	% of Total HH
Television/ Radio / VCR	723	100.0
Cell phone (mobile phone)	319	44.2
Satellite Dish	161	22.3
Clothes Iron	134	18.5
Bedroom suite	115	15.9
Motor vehicle	114	15.8
Deep freeze/ Refrigerator	226	31.3
Tape Player	97	13.4
Microwave	95	13.1
Personal Computer	92	12.7
Hi-fi music centre	87	12.0
Sewing machine	86	11.9
Hotplate	84	11.6
Telephone in house	81	11.2
Bicycle	79	10.9
Fan / Air-conditioner/ heater	122	16.9
Stove (gas/ paraffin/ primers)	45	6.2
Cattle/goats/pigs/sheep	85	11.8
Poultry	33	4.6
Personal financial banking products	30	4.1
Plough	25	3.5
Solar panels	24	3.3
Electric washing machine	23	3.2
Minibus	20	2.8
Cooler box	17	2.4
Generator	15	2.1
Fields	13	1.8
Donkeys/horses	10	1.4
Tractor	7	1.0
Motorbike	6	0.8
Plastic drums	4	0.6
Bakkie	3	0.4
Other items	88	12.2
No items bought	12	1.7

Despite the harsh macro-economic climate currently prevailing in the country, most households indicated that they had some savings. Households had managed to save an average of R1,621 from remittance transfers in the year prior to the survey. In total, only 9.5% of households said they had no savings (Table 33). Most that save in Zimbabwe or in other countries have their money in banks.

Table 33: Household Savings			
		No.	% of Households
Type of Savings	Savings at home	241	26.2
	Savings in own country	480	55.6
	Savings in other country	81	9.4
	No savings	79	8.8
N = 881			
Location of Savings		No.	%
Savings at Home	Friends	11	4.6
	Family	29	12.0
	Savings group	4	1.7
	Post Office	2	0.8
	Burial society	2	0.8
	Bank	177	73.4
	Church	5	2.1
	Other	10	4.1
	Don't know	1	0.4
	Total	241	100.0
Savings in Own Country	Friends	3	0.6
	Family	8	1.7
	Savings group	4	0.8
	Post Office	3	0.6
	Burial society	22	4.6
	Bank	433	90.2
	Other	4	0.8
	Don't know	3	0.6
	Total	480	100.0
Savings in Other Country	Family	3	3.7
	Bank	65	80.2
	Church	1	1.2
	Other	9	11.1
	Don't know	3	3.7
	Total	81	100.0

Migrants tend to send more money when the family falls on hard times or needs emergency funds for funerals or feasts. On average, migrants contributed R264 to meet the cost of the most recent emergency or special event. The migrants also sent goods for use during these events including coffins in case of bereavement, groceries and food. The mean value of the goods sent for the most recent special event was R100.

CONCLUSION

Remittances are an essential part of household budgets and the national economy of Zimbabwe. In recent years, remittance flows have increased due to the growing number of Zimbabwean migrants who transfer cash and goods through both formal and informal channels. These informal transfer systems include sending remittances through relatives, friends, trusted agents and personal transport of cash or goods. Other informal transport services operate as side business to an import-export operation, retail shop or currency dealership. More recently the internet has begun to be used to transfer remittances.

The MARS study shows that remittances are mostly used for basic consumption (e.g. for food, school fees, medical expenses and for building). A small number of households have been able to use their remittances to increase income through purchase and sale of goods or in investment in transportation or farming. Remittances are certainly spent on luxury goods but with the exception of cell phones and some electronic equipment, only a small minority of households can afford to spend very much on these goods. What is interesting is that households do try and save a portion of their remittances although it is likely that any value that savings had in 2005 would have been wiped out by rampant inflation.

The study clearly shows that without remittance flows, the situation of many Zimbabwean households would be even more dire than it is already. Remittances have reduced vulnerability to hunger, ill-health and poverty in both rural and urban households. A comparison with randomly selected households shows that households with migrants go without basic necessities less often. Remittances also allow families to keep children in school and to put roofs over the heads of household members. There is a double irony here. Without the economic crisis in Zimbabwe, migration would not have reached the volume that it has. In turn, migration (through remittances) has staved off the worst aspects of that crisis for many households, and even kept the national economy afloat (if only barely). However, the depth of the crisis and the struggle for survival mean that remittances are rarely used in a systematic or sustained manner for what might broadly be called "developmental" purposes. That is not why migrants remit and those are not the uses to which remittances are put.

ENDNOTES

1   S. Maimbo and D. Ratha, Eds, *Remittances: Development Impact and Future Prospects* (Washington, DC: World Bank, 2005); World Bank, *Global Economic Prospects Economic Implications of Remittances and Migration* (Washington: The World Bank, 2006); Ç. Özden, and M. Schiff, Eds, *International Migration, Remittances, and the Brain Drain* (Washington: World Bank, 2006); R. Vargas-Lundius, G. Lanly, M. Villareal and M. Osorio, *International Migration, Remittances and Rural Development* (Rome: IFAD/FAO, 2008).

2   M. Orozco, "Conceptual Considerations, Empirical Challenges and Solutions in Measuring Remittances" Report for Inter-American Dialogue, 2006.

3   Existing studies of remittance flows to Zimbabwe tend to focus on case-study evidence: see S. Bracking and L. Sachikonye, *Remittances, Poverty Reduction and the Informalisation of Household Wellbeing in Zimbabwe*, Global Poverty Research Group, Working Paper No. 45, 2006; F. Maphosa, "Remittances and Development: The Impact of Migration to South Africa on Rural Livelihoods in Southern Zimbabwe" *Development Southern Africa* 24 (1) (2007): 123-36; F. Magunha, A. Bailey and L. Cliffe, "Remittance Strategies of Zimbabweans in Northern England" School of Geography, University of Leeds, Leeds, 2009.

4   For regional overviews see W. Pendleton, J. Crush, E. Campbell, T. Green, H. Simelane, D. Tevera and F. de Vletter, "Migration, Remittances and Development in Southern Africa" SAMP Migration Policy Series No. 44, Cape Town, 2006; B. Dodson with H. Simelane, D. Tevera, T. Green, A. Chikanda and F. de Vletter, "Gender, Migration and Remittances in Southern Africa" SAMP Migration Policy Series No. 49, Cape Town, 2008.

5   G. Foster, C. Mafuka, R. Drew and E. Kravolec, "Factors Leading to the Establishment of Child-Headed Households" *Health Transition Review* 7 (1997): 155-68; G. Bicego, J. Boerma and C. Carine, "The Effect of AIDS on Maternal Mortality in Malawi and Zimbabwe" *AIDS* 16 (7) (2002): 1078-81.

6   A. Bloch, "Zimbabweans in Britain: Transnational Activities and Capabilities" *Journal of Ethnic and Migration Studies* 34(2) (2008): 287-305.

7   At the time of the survey, the official exchange rate was 1US$ to 6,042Z$, while at the parallel market, the rate was about 1US$ to Z$8,338.

8   The weighted value is calculated by multiplying the number of cases 'N' by the median household value. The median value is a more reliable measure since the mean is often distorted by a small number of large values.

9   The Lived Poverty Index (LPI) was developed by Afrobarometer and used in their country studies. Robert Mattes provided information on the LPI and gave permission for its use in the MARS project. For more on the LPI see R. Mattes, M. Bratton and Y. Davids, "Poverty, Survival and Democracy in Southern Africa" Afrobarometer Working Paper No. 23, 2003.

10 The Afrobarometer Network, "Afrobarometer Round 2: Compendium of Comparative Results from a 15-Country Survey" Afrobarometer Working Paper No. 34, 2004.

11 R. Mattes, M. Bratton and Y. Davids, "Poverty, Survival and Democracy in Southern Africa," Afrobarometer Working Paper No. 23, 2003.

12 L. B. Landau, "Drowning in Numbers: Interrogating New Patterns of Zimbabwean Migration to South Africa," Briefing prepared for Centre for Development and Enterprise, 2007.

13 See for example Daniel Tevera and Jonathan Crush, "The New Brain Drain from Zimbabwe" SAMP Migration Policy Series No. 29, Cape Town, 2003; Daniel Tevera, "Early Departures: The Emigration Potential of Zimbabwean Students" SAMP Migration Policy Series No. 39, Cape Town, 2005.

14 K. Newland, "Migration as a Factor in Development and Poverty Reduction: The Impact of Rich Countries' Immigration Policies on the Prospects of the Poor" In R. Picciotto and R. Weaving, Eds, *Impact of Rich Countries' Policies on Poor Countries* (New Brunswick, NJ: Transaction, 2004), pp. 194-5; H. de Haas, "International Migration, Remittances and Development: Myths and Fact" Global Migration Perspectives No. 30 (Geneva: GCIM, 2005).

MIGRATION POLICY SERIES

1. *Covert Operations: Clandestine Migration, Temporary Work and Immigration Policy in South Africa* (1997) ISBN 1-874864-51-9

2. *Riding the Tiger: Lesotho Miners and Permanent Residence in South Africa* (1997) ISBN 1-874864-52-7

3. *International Migration, Immigrant Entrepreneurs and South Africa's Small Enterprise Economy* (1997) ISBN 1-874864-62-4

4. *Silenced by Nation Building: African Immigrants and Language Policy in the New South Africa* (1998) ISBN 1-874864-64-0

5. *Left Out in the Cold? Housing and Immigration in the New South Africa* (1998) ISBN 1-874864-68-3

6. *Trading Places: Cross-Border Traders and the South African Informal Sector* (1998) ISBN 1-874864-71-3

7. *Challenging Xenophobia: Myth and Realities about Cross-Border Migration in Southern Africa* (1998) ISBN 1-874864-70-5

8. *Sons of Mozambique: Mozambican Miners and Post-Apartheid South Africa* (1998) ISBN 1-874864-78-0

9. *Women on the Move: Gender and Cross-Border Migration to South Africa* (1998) ISBN 1-874864-82-9.

10. *Namibians on South Africa: Attitudes Towards Cross-Border Migration and Immigration Policy* (1998) ISBN 1-874864-84-5.

11. *Building Skills: Cross-Border Migrants and the South African Construction Industry* (1999) ISBN 1-874864-84-5

12. *Immigration & Education: International Students at South African Universities and Technikons* (1999) ISBN 1-874864-89-6

13. *The Lives and Times of African Immigrants in Post-Apartheid South Africa* (1999) ISBN 1-874864-91-8

14. *Still Waiting for the Barbarians: South African Attitudes to Immigrants and Immigration* (1999) ISBN 1-874864-91-8
15. *Undermining Labour: Migrancy and Sub-contracting in the South African Gold Mining Industry* (1999) ISBN 1-874864-91-8
16. *Borderline Farming: Foreign Migrants in South African Commercial Agriculture* (2000) ISBN 1-874864-97-7
17. *Writing Xenophobia: Immigration and the Press in Post-Apartheid South Africa* (2000) ISBN 1-919798-01-3
18. *Losing Our Minds: Skills Migration and the South African Brain Drain* (2000) ISBN 1-919798-03-x
19. *Botswana: Migration Perspectives and Prospects* (2000) ISBN 1-919798-04-8
20. *The Brain Gain: Skilled Migrants and Immigration Policy in Post-Apartheid South Africa* (2000) ISBN 1-919798-14-5
21. *Cross-Border Raiding and Community Conflict in the Lesotho-South African Border Zone* (2001) ISBN 1-919798-16-1
22. *Immigration, Xenophobia and Human Rights in South Africa* (2001) ISBN 1-919798-30-7
23. *Gender and the Brain Drain from South Africa* (2001) ISBN 1-919798-35-8
24. *Spaces of Vulnerability: Migration and HIV/AIDS in South Africa* (2002) ISBN 1-919798-38-2
25. *Zimbabweans Who Move: Perspectives on International Migration in Zimbabwe* (2002) ISBN 1-919798-40-4
26. *The Border Within: The Future of the Lesotho-South African International Boundary* (2002) ISBN 1-919798-41-2
27. *Mobile Namibia: Migration Trends and Attitudes* (2002) ISBN 1-919798-44-7
28. *Changing Attitudes to Immigration and Refugee Policy in Botswana* (2003) ISBN 1-919798-47-1
29. *The New Brain Drain from Zimbabwe* (2003) ISBN 1-919798-48-X
30. *Regionalizing Xenophobia? Citizen Attitudes to Immigration and Refugee Policy in Southern Africa* (2004) ISBN 1-919798-53-6
31. *Migration, Sexuality and HIV/AIDS in Rural South Africa* (2004) ISBN 1-919798-63-3
32. *Swaziland Moves: Perceptions and Patterns of Modern Migration* (2004) ISBN 1-919798-67-6
33. *HIV/AIDS and Children's Migration in Southern Africa* (2004) ISBN 1-919798-70-6
34. *Medical Leave: The Exodus of Health Professionals from Zimbabwe* (2005) ISBN 1-919798-74-9
35. *Degrees of Uncertainty: Students and the Brain Drain in Southern Africa* (2005) ISBN 1-919798-84-6
36. *Restless Minds: South African Students and the Brain Drain* (2005) ISBN 1-919798-82-X
37. *Understanding Press Coverage of Cross-Border Migration in Southern Africa since 2000* (2005) ISBN 1-919798-91-9

38. *Northern Gateway: Cross-Border Migration Between Namibia and Angola* (2005) ISBN 1-919798-92-7
39. *Early Departures: The Emigration Potential of Zimbabwean Students* (2005) ISBN 1-919798-99-4
40. *Migration and Domestic Workers: Worlds of Work, Health and Mobility in Johannesburg* (2005) ISBN 1-920118-02-0
41. *The Quality of Migration Services Delivery in South Africa* (2005) ISBN 1-920118-03-9
42. *States of Vulnerability: The Future Brain Drain of Talent to South Africa* (2006) ISBN 1-920118-07-1
43. *Migration and Development in Mozambique: Poverty, Inequality and Survival* (2006) ISBN 1-920118-10-1
44. *Migration, Remittances and Development in Southern Africa* (2006) ISBN 1-920118-15-2
45. *Medical Recruiting: The Case of South African Health Care Professionals* (2007) ISBN 1-920118-47-0
46. *Voices From the Margins: Migrant Women's Experiences in Southern Africa* (2007) ISBN 1-920118-50-0
47. *The Haemorrhage of Health Professionals From South Africa: Medical Opinions* (2007) ISBN 978-1-920118-63-1
48. *The Quality of Immigration and Citizenship Services in Namibia* (2008) ISBN 978-1-920118-67-9
49. *Gender, Migration and Remittances in Southern Africa* (2008) ISBN 978-1-920118-70-9
50. *The Perfect Storm: The Realities of Xenophobia in Contemporary South Africa* (2008) ISBN 978-1-920118-71-6

www.ingramcontent.com/pod-product-compliance
Lightning Source LLC
Chambersburg PA
CBHW080428270326
41929CB00018B/3202